destiny called her name

A COLLECTION OF POETRY

LINDSEY ANDERSON

Dedication

I dedicate this book to my parents, Michael and Vicki, and my two beautiful daughters, Olivia and Grace. I love each of you more than words could ever describe. Writing this book has allowed me to heal some of my past hurts and given me hope for tomorrow. May we all have nothing but bright days ahead of us.

Here's to the future.

TABLE OF CONTENTS

chapter three

CHAPTER ONE

the creation of love

There's a special love inside me, buried deep within my soul. It's something you can't see, hear or touch...a sort of invisible feeling.

The only way you can get what I have inside of me, is to have someone as special as I do, to create that spark so love can grow, like a fire enveloping- getting bigger and expanding.

Soon, so uncontrollable, not a single soul could put out this force holding natural powers which we don't understand or even try to.

We will never know how love works, or even if answers exist. A question already answered by knowing the unknown.

People's unique love fitting together with others as to make a match or pair. A puzzle needing that special piece to be complete. We create love, not carry it as a possession.

Knowing that I have a special love that I helped create gives me a feeling of importance.

Something I worked at so hard, even when finding that missing puzzle piece lost in my heart seemed impossible, I never gave up.

For the love I wanted so desperately is what kept me going.

A theory I believed as true may be viewed as a false truth by others.

Going through this process, which is ignored and unseen, is the only way an understanding will ever be met.

These are the feelings I hold inside of me.

Hoping you now understand the journey I take to receive your love.

Something so special, no money could buy.

Now, when the person you love must leave this world,
you must carry on, always knowing that the fire burning inside
of you will never be put out.

You keep the love until one day you can share it again.

For they did not take the love back and give it to another, they
simply locked it inside your heart knowing that it is the only
truly safe place for it to be.

There is no lock strong enough to hold this priceless
possession we call love.

destiny

Once in your life, you will meet a soul
so in tune to yours,
connected in ways like never before.
Sparks fly with the littlest kiss.
Each time your eyes meet,
all you can see is sunshine.
In their arms, you are at home.

soulmates

From the moment you came in my life,
my heart has been locked in your hand.
I dream of one day being your wife,
and am praying, that is God's plan.

Your children are the reasons,
I fell in love with you.
Through pictures I could see for them,
there is nothing you wouldn't do.

From the very first day,
I knew you were different from the rest.
We had so much to say,
and even secrets to confess.

You cried to me for hours,
about losing your best friend.
I knew from that day forward,
your broken heart I was to mend.

We are so connected,
in a way I can't explain.
We hear each other's thoughts,
and even feel each other's pain.

When one of us is hurting,
the other feels it too.
There's never need for secrets,
because we both know what we do.

Never have I felt,
more at home than in your arms.
You give me love like no one has,
and keep me safe from harm.

Now I'm looking out this window,
on my way to you.
Soon I'll be in your arms,
you're my dream come true.

divine timing

From the moment I
looked into your eyes
my soul knew you
were the one
I had been searching
for my entire life.
Your soul was
my home and my
heart was yours
once again.
We traveled through
space and time,
incarnated over
lifetimes that
brought us together
for eternity.

XOXOXO

You press your lips against mine.
I'm suspended in the air.
There's no rhyme or reason
to this secret love affair.
You kiss my neck,
then navel to toes.
I can feel you inside me already,
but I'm still wearing all my clothes.
You look me in my eyes,
So deep and dark they shine.
I can't help but smile at you,
You're just so God damn fine.
Now we're naked skin to skin,
And you put your love inside.
You never knew the reason
Each time we made love I cried.
Loving you is more painful
Than any burn, cut or bruise-
All I ever wanted was to be the
Only one you choose.
I'm lost without you near me,
I'm empty while you're away.
Please if you say anything at all,
Just promise me you'll say....
... "I love you baby more than life itself,
I'll never let you go."
That's all I need to be complete.
XOXOXO

bleed

He peeled back
my layers,
one by one,
careful not to
make me bleed.

hopeless

Keeping them apart would be as utterly hopeless as separating the ocean waves from the sandy shore..... you can't have one without the other.

beautiful

He made her feel beautiful—
more than any mirror ever had.
Having his love made her priceless for the first time.
Before him, she never realized her worth.

mirror souls

I didn't imagine the feelings.
You can't fake something so real.
Just one touch of your hand on
my thigh along with those looks
your eyes can't conceal.

Our bodies charged like they're
magnets.
Our auras glowing bright green.
The second they leave us alone in
a room is the moment we live in a
dream.

The chemistry between us
explosive.
This fires burning out of control.
We can't take for granted
this chance as twin flames
to awaken and heal our souls.

music to my soul

Your love is like music to my ears...
i can't stop listening...
...can't stop thinking about your hands,
so strong and beautifully calloused.
The imperfections on your face
more attractive than your perfect smile...
the depth your eyes carry
a vast universe lies beneath them.
I can see stars and infinite galaxies...
Your soul screams like music
I've never heard..
tastes like pleasure
I've never dreamt existed.
You are perfect...
Every inch of your body,
every piece of you...
like a handmade quilt passed on
for generations acquiring more value over time.
I love you... To infinity and beyond.
You are mine for every lifetime we exist,
you are mine for all of time.

my twin

You inspire me to be, the best version of myself.
You fill my soul, and set my spirit free.
You let me be, just who I am, and love me unconditionally.
Each time I see you, I can't help but smile,
you are my happy place.
I can't imagine living without, waking up to your smiling face.
I have dreams of a future, where lies don't exist;
heartache and pain are no more.
There's something much better,
you just have to believe, that it's worth fighting for.

deep inside

Not a moment goes by,
that you don't cross my mind.
My imagination runs wild.
Dreams of soft whispers,
follow nights of lovemaking.
Erotic fantasies fulfilled.
Intimate secrets we are eager
to share, disappear
when light floods the room.
Sunrise brings jealousy who
tells my heart I'm just a fool.
Darkness invites the moon to
orchestrate my dreams.
This love is chaos at its finest.
Beautiful, unbreakable,
charismatic.
Our souls intertwined,
dancing in the dark,
to a rhythm only we know.

bloom

You changed me.
I can finally be the woman I was
created to be.
Water me.
Watch me bloom like a rose.
Flourish in my new-found soil.

kissing the sky

Last night I dreamt of you.
We were flying in a hot air balloon.
The view was unexplainable- remarkable actually.
The higher we traveled, the closer heaven became.
We were free.
Free to enjoy the wind, as it carried us far above
the earth.
Nothing mattered anymore.
For a moment in time we were both traveling at the
same speed.
We were free.
Distance between us vanished.
The look in your eyes I will never forget.
I've never felt so close to you.
In my dreams, we are free.

sword in hand

My knight in shining armor.
You rode in with sword in hand
and rescued me from the darkness.
My world became beautiful.
Troubles became obsolete.
Fears dissipated.
Dreams materialized.
Transformation was inevitable.
You saved me... from myself.

infinite love

Across oceans that go on for thousands of miles,
through tundra, rainforests and snow.
Through all of these I'd travel just so, in your
heart you would always know.
That the light in your eyes could blind the very
soul your heart desires,
while the spark you ignite each time that you
smile could start catastrophic fires.
There isn't a star that could light up the sky
brighter than your auras glow,
and no spaceship that could travel farther than
my love for you could go.

in between the sheets

I crave the scent of your skin,
the way it lingers after you
loved on my body all night.
I get goosebumps just
thinking about your lips
gently kissing the nape
of my neck, while you wrap
my hair around your fist
and pull ever so slightly.
Our legs twisted like
pretzels as we play
in between the sheets.

your love is like a tattoo

I am staring up at the moon and the only thing I can think about is you.
I see your face in the clouds- you are smiling.
My life feels so pointless without you next to me- my heart hurts.
I can't help but wonder if you are thinking of me too.
Waiting for my phone to ring, wishing the next text was from you.
Your love is like a tattoo- it hurts sometimes but leaves a mark that will last forever.
I pray every night for you to visit me in my dreams.
That is the only way I can have you all the time.
I know it won't always be this hard.
Please don't ever let go.
You are my future.
I love you.

sweet like honey

I'm screaming out your name.
Yet you fail to listen, miserably.
You were the air in my lungs last summer.
I can still feel every kiss goodnight.
The memories flood my mind.
I'm running in circles looking for you,
yet I'm standing ever so still.
I want to feel alive again.
Merely existing is not my cup of tea.
I want bliss and sunshine in my face.
Daffodils and tulips covering the ground
beneath my feet.
Kisses that taste sweet like honey.
The kind only your lips can give.

CHAPTER TWO

magic cloud

As I lie here staring at the moon and the stars,
I think only of your smiling face.
Not of the wounds or the scars, just of a beautiful place.
A place in the sky, so big and bright, there's no lies or time to
fight. Just loving and caring, no yelling or swearing, and for a
moment in time, everything is just right.
All who is there, just you and I,
with a beautiful view of the moon in the sky.
We are dancing and floating on a magic cloud, but there's no
music, or screams from a crowd.
We are all alone and not fighting for a change,
but during our perfect moment, it begins to rain.
A huge storm comes upon us, and each other we try to blame-
but it doesn't work.
We are stuck on this cloud, with nowhere to go- we must work
this out, or love together we will never know.
We must come to a decision on who will win- you or I?
Do we blame it on each other, or call it a tie?
I have an idea, on what we must do-
we must change this dark cloud beneath us to a clear, bright
blue. Make it realize this isn't your fault or mine,
and have it carry us to a place I long to find...LOVE.

entitled

Instead of demanding the love I'm entitled to-
the love I deserved, I settled for any little piece of his heart
I could get my hands on, with the hope that if I gathered enough
pieces over time, that eventually I would have the entire thing...
oh how wrong I was.

painful truth

I keep telling myself I'm okay living without you.
Not sure why I feel the need to lie to myself of all people.
I am anything BUT okay.
I want to be the woman you hurry home to after work.
The one you think of when you smell an amazing bottle of
perfume.
I want to be the warmth you crave each night when bedtime
crawls near.
But reality is I'm none of those things to you.
I guess you could say I've been living in Dreamland.
I was so sure you were the one I had been waiting for my
entire life.
Now I question everything I do, everyone I thought meant
something to me.
Maybe I don't know anything except just that.
I would give anything to know that I meant to you even a
fraction of what you mean to me.
Somehow that little bit of knowing helps.
Because everyday, I am reminded that I never knew you, and
quite possibly, you never knew me.

a prayer for broken hearts

They say time heals a broken heart- my wounds would disagree.
I knew I loved you from the start- whoever said love was free?
Never knowing where I stand- my whole life I've been lost.
Empty dreams that once were full- I can't afford the cost.
Memories of good times, are few and far between.
Fairytales of knights in armor, were never what they seemed.
Black roses with thorns, replaced red petals and long stems.
Man made stones and gold plate, instead of precious gems.
It's not fair to make me wait, my love for you is true.
The only way to mend my heart, is if it's loved by you.
Promise you will love me, until your dying day.
Wipe these tears, as I cry, and kneel with me as I pray.
Dear God we come as one, but started off as two.
Our broken souls and shattered dreams,
brought us straight to you.
We lift up your name, as we raise our arms to praise.
Our Lord and savior Jesus Christ, the creator of our days.
Amen.

you should know

Just when I thought I'd never see you again,
you came by to say hello.
I regret all the times, I prayed for this day,
because it hurt even more to watch you go.
I thought if I got to touch you,
even just one more time,
I'd be satisfied with just one kiss.
But no matter how much time or how little
I get, each second without you I miss.
There are so many things I wanted to say,
but I just didn't know quite how.
Like how each time, I look in your eyes,
I see love that can't exist now.
My soul was screaming "I need you!"
and "please don't ever let go!"
But now you are gone, and so is my chance,
to tell you these things I think you should know.

heartless

We found each other somewhere
between infinity and never.
You filled my heart so full of love it
exploded- and left me heartless.

my missing piece

When one person
can make you realize,
that before them,
you were never whole,
a sense of disbelief
comes over you.
Your entire existence
becomes questionable.
And how was it even
possible that you were now,
after this realization,
living alone,
as if it was only meant to
teach you some sort of lesson?
As if I needed another broken heart.
If I would have known that
finding my missing piece
was going to destroy all my other pieces,
I would of settled for being one shy.

pieces of you

Absence makes the heart grow
fonder- at least that's what they say.
Waking up without you, gets harder
each and every day.
Daydreams about the warmth of our
next kiss- will we close our eyes?
Fantasies of making love under
moonlit star-filled skies.
Memories of heartache, and who we
used to be, fade like old pictures
that we were never meant to see.
Minute by minute, my heart beats for
your touch.
For me to be the only one, am I ask-
ing for too much?
Baby, I NEED YOU more than you'll
ever know- but just like a flower
needs water, we need love to grow.
How will we ever know if we were
meant to be?
Give me all of you RIGHT NOW- if not,
then set me free.

your golden stair

Why am I so desperate to see you?
What more can I learn from your eyes?
They've already shown me your weakness.
They've never watched as I cried.

Why do I long just to hold you?
What more of your body haven't I seen?
You never are close when I need you.
You should only say what you mean.

When do we get to be honest?
Will we ever not live in a lie?
At what point does our love not feel broken?
Are you ever going to try?

At times giving up seems like the answer.
Then there are days I can't bear the thought.
Am I supposed to keep waiting?
What happens if we should get caught?

I need you to know that I LOVE YOU.
PLEASE show me that you still care.
If you ever look and can't find me,
I'll leave my heart at your golden stair.

my perfect person

Each morning I wake up without you,
I can't even open my eyes.
The tears just won't stop falling,
My heart drowns from the cries.
Yesterday I needed you near me,
Tomorrow I'll long for your touch.
Today I pray that God hears me,
I don't think I'm asking too much.
All I want is to love you,
And make you smile everyday.
Never put anyone above you,
Or let anything get in our way.
This isn't going to be easy,
But I know if we truly care,
We can build up each other,
It won't matter who else is there.
I'm asking you to forgive me,
I said some things I didn't mean,
Please accept my apology,
It's not as hard as it seems.
I hope one day that you read this,
Knowing I'll always be your friend.
Until that day I'll tell Jesus,
In case I never see you again.

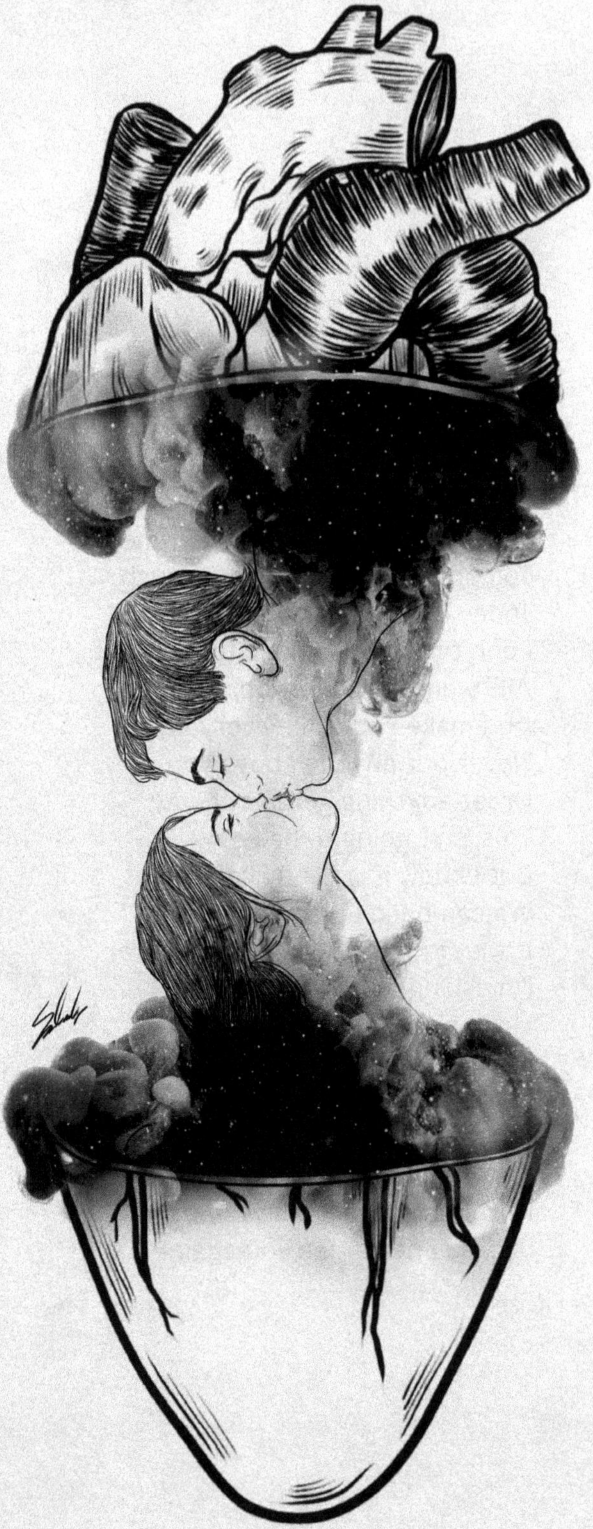

a kiss goodbye

I didn't even get a kiss goodbye.
You broke my heart in two.
I'm empty wondering why.
My soul aches for your presence.
If only I could touch you.
I long to feel your warmth.
Nobody else could ever compare.
You were my favorite.
I still love you with my broken heart.

poor soul

Nobody has ever left me so empty as you. To think my heart so full of love was nothing to you but poisonous venom. I gave you my love so freely, I didn't even need to bite your flesh. The moment my love touched your soul you died from the wealth in my veins.

more than you know

Why do I still love you like you never said goodbye?
Why can't my heart let you go?
When will these tears stop falling like rain?
I'd give anything just to know.
I go to bed each night alone,
And cry myself to sleep.
Nothing ever changes though,
Hours turn to days, then weeks.
Month after month, I'm still lost without you.
Tomorrow it's been a year since we met.
You kissed me under the stars and held me in your arms,
That night I will never forget.
You couldn't wait to see me,
You couldn't even wait a minute more.
Now I have dreams about what it would be like to see you
walking through my door.
I don't think you will ever understand the way that I feel,
I'm beyond a little heartbroken,
I don't think I'm ever going to heal.

the end

For a moment in time, my life felt complete-
being in your arms was like a dream.
How am I supposed to go on without you?
You were joy, love, happiness, and strength
all bundled into one.
Each day was a gift- opening my eyes each
morning was like being a child on Christmas Day.
My doubts were no more, my pain was erased.
Now all you see are tears running down my face.
My dreams turned dark, my hopes became weak.
Now I'm lost and don't want to be found.
Running through a maze, with walls ten feet high-
screaming "is anybody there!?"
"Hello, does anybody care?"
Nobody ever answers- unless they whisper lies.
Time keeps dragging on.
There is no simple answer, no easy fix.
If I have to exist without you by my side,
I may as well be dead.
You were keeping me alive.

without you

I always pay attention to my surroundings.
I know better, than to let my guard down.
I failed to see you coming.
I failed to stop n' look around.
You took all the time that you needed.
It was too easy, for you to creep in.
I hate that I was the reason you cheated,
I hate that I wonder what could've been.
I'm not sure if I am more empty,
Now, or before we crossed paths.
It's hard to sit and hear silence,
When my heart, still listens for your laugh.
I erased all the photos of you,
To ease the pain, each time I look in your eyes,
My mind, won't erase the image of your face, no
matter how hard I try.
I know, you can feel when I'm hurting,
I know, in a way, it hurts you too.
If only, we would of met sooner,
I wouldn't be forced, to live, without you.

on repeat

I loved you then. I love you still. My broken heart sings of you. I'm dying to know you still care. I let you get the best of me. You were selfish to never say goodbye. How expensive it is to hold onto you. My mind replays our moments over and over... on repeat.

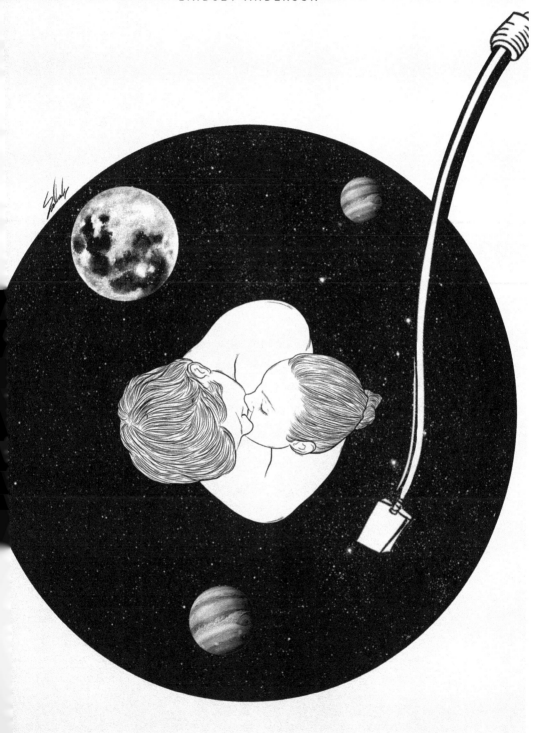

no words

Desperate to put a label on the
emptiness I feel without you.
Wishing the paper would absorb
my pain and set me free...
...but there are no words to express
the weight I bear from your absence.

you

Living without you is like
waking up to a rainy day-
I just look out the
window waiting for the
sun to appear from
behind the dark clouds. It
seems so pointless going
through life unhappy.
Like no matter what I
accomplish, or where I
go, or who I see- none
of it really matters too
much. Because you
weren't part of it.
You weren't there to
share the moment with.
Whether it was eating
pizza and watching the
game, or going out to a
movie.
Everything and nothing
are pretty much all I
know these days.
Everything sucks
without you and nothing
feels right with anyone
else....

killing me softly

Thoughts of you flood my mind. I can't escape my realities fate.
Searching for love I can't find, my heart must patiently wait.
Visions of you drowning my soul, whispers of love-making sin.
Fantasies out of control, when will this pain ever end?
Wishes fade slow like the sun, as the jealous moon starts to rise.
Like bullets jammed in a gun, love is pains perfect disguise.

what dreaming can do

Here I am, heartbroken and torn-
you promised me you'de always stay true.
Life is pointless without your love,
God please tell me what to do.
I can't begin to explain how this feels,
the emptiness flows through my veins.
The air outside, so cold it brings chills-
The only sound is falling rain.
You came into my life, like a breath of fresh air,
wrapping my soul with your love.
Each time that you leave, I wait with hope
you'll return,
like an angel sent from heaven above.
How do I let these feelings subside,
now that your love owns my heart?
It's never enough to have you by my side,
because what comes next is pain when we part.
I'm torn between two worlds that aren't
always as they seem.
When I heard your soul say "I love you"...
... that's when I woke from my dream.

invisible

What I wouldn't give, to hold you in my arms,
and feel your heartbeat next to mine.

Just to know you're thinking of me too-
If only you would stop and take some time.

I'm all alone and secretly I'm dying from the pain.
I fake a smile all day long, and it's driving me insane.

If only I could make you see, just how much I care.
But my loves invisible, it vanished in thin air.

shattered dreams

I hate the way I feel.
I'm so tired of the pain.
It hurts waking up alone.
It's driving me insane.
Promises don't mean shit.
Truth is just a pretty lie.
I should of known better.
Instead I chose to cry.
Time after time, I thought I found the one.
Then you came and started something
that can never be undone.
You made me feel alive and free.
All my pain went away.
Now I'm locked behind closed doors.
Now there's nothing u can say.
I know I'll never have you,
the way I thought I would.
These shattered dreams won't let
me sleep even if they could.

distance

Destiny lied when it told me you were FOREVER.
My heart still shattered in pieces from the impact.
Words can't describe the depth pain travels
when your heart is the destination.

stay awhile

How many times, can a human heart break,
before it's too much to repair?
They say what doesn't kill us makes us stronger,
but to me it just doesn't seem fair.
Why do I always get the short end of the stick,
when all I ever wanted was to be loved?
Maybe I'm not meant to wear a wedding gown,
like the ones I've always dreamed of.
If only I could figure out exactly where I went wrong,
so I don't make that wrong turn again.
I'd give anything, to turn back time,
and just be grateful we had stayed friends.
My heart is like an open book,
it doesn't hide how I feel.
There isn't enough money on Earth,
that could buy a love more real.
It's hard to be in my shoes,
when I'm forced to fake a smile.
I hope one day I'll find someone,
who wants to stay awhile...

vanishing act

Each second that passes, is a sparkle in your eyes
I can't see. Each minute that goes by, will soon be
nothing more than history. For every hour I have to
miss you, there's a thousand I love yous inside.
For the time it takes to forget you each day, there's
a million tears I have cried.
I tell you about all my feelings, when I know better,
it's true. I swear I'll never text again, but the first
one in my outbox is inevitably you.
I lie and say I hate you for the weak woman that
I've become. I trade my soul to the devil each time I
pray you'll tell me I'm the one. I can't stand to pass a
mirror that looks me in my eyes.
It's just like you it's says I'm fine and feeds me full of
lies. I wish I could do magic, and pull you right out of
a hat. I'd use you for a laugh or two and poof you'd
go right back. Then we both would have a magic
wand to make you disappear, only yours is not the
kind like mine, or at least that's what I hear.
Next time you work your magic, and twirl your little
stick, think twice before you break a heart with fake
love disguised as dick.

be still my heart

I'm still living without you.
Your face, your memory burned in my
mind. I'm scarred, forever missing your
touch. You made me feel beautiful, more
than any mirror ever had.
Possibilities were endless while laying in
your arms.
You completed me.
Be still my heart.

promises

I don't even know how to tell you,
all the things I wanted to say.
Before you walked out of my life,
after my feelings just got in the way.

None of this has been easy,
I'd be lying to say I don't care.
I hate feeling so empty,
but this life just isn't fair.

No choice but to keep going,
I can't get lost in the pain.
The sun outside is shining,
but all I keep seeing is rain.

Promises aren't meant to be broken,
love has a mind of its own.
No truer words have been spoken,
I've never felt so alone.

I can still taste the kisses you loaned me,
but can't return the looks in your eyes.
I'll never know truth as it should be,
when all my ears know are lies.

truth hurts

I wasn't ready to be loved by you.
I didn't even know life before our eyes met.
You took me on a journey to a place where
love and fear collide.
I wasn't ready to be loved by you.
I had been broken in the past.
Blinded by love so sweet.
Past any barrier flesh would conceal.
My hopes overflowing in vain.
I wasn't ready to be loved by you.
Truth hurts.

rehab

You are the only one who knows, exactly
how I feel- I can't get you out of my mind.
The way you look in my eyes can't conceal,
the real love you are struggling to find.

We met for a reason, and only God knows
why- this wasn't part of his plan.
You showed me your heart, and in the blink
of an eye, you took my love and ran.

Overflowing with emptiness, tears falling
like rain- why did you have to leave?
I begin to reminisce, I can't take the pain,
and it's making it hard to breathe.

There's something about you, that's so
hard to forget- you're like a drug and I'm
the fiend. You got me strung out, now I'm
having withdrawals- I'm afraid it's time to
get clean.

lost in love

Words can't describe the way you make me feel,
I'm empty without your touch.

Never has my heart felt something so real,
I never knew I could love someone so much.

In your arms I feel complete,
only now I know I was never whole.

Dear God how am I supposed to live,
without the other half of my soul?

Accepting my truth or living a lie,
these are the choices I face.

It doesn't do any good to try,
and forget what can't be erased.

I hope you know just how much
your love has helped me grow.

I've learned that when you truly
love someone is when you let them go.

the waiting game

I waited for your love, for the very last time.
Picked up a pen in hopes I could write the pain away.
No words that could describe the depth in a rhyme,
Not a vowel that I could buy to make you stay.
This is the part where I let you go,
To see how much you really care.
I'll set you free, but for now just know,
It killed me inside to keep playing along
when we both know the rules aren't fair.

love myself more

Instead of shutting you out, I choose to leave the
door open for you. No locks, no keys. No walls
to climb or windows to break. I simply let go of the
illusion of control. You come and go as you
please these days, no goodbyes or farewells. I'm no
longer surprised when I see you've shown
up. I could be angry- even furious maybe. But today
I am going to be free from the burden your
absence places upon me, I'm not going to cover up
the pain with makeup or douse the
heartache with perfume. Today I'm going to say
"hello" if I'm graced with your presence...
Yesterday I was full of self pity and bitterness.
Today, I LOVE MYSELF MORE.... MORE THAN
I EVER THOUGHT YOU LOVED ME, MORE THAN I
EVER KNEW I LOVED YOU.

CHAPTER THREE

my reflection

Painful eyes, full of doubt and despair.
The mirror can't hide or conceal the emptiness...
Silent glass screaming so loud with vengeance,
what a pitiful sight to see.
Bitter truth forced so hastily down my throat,
leaving me no choice but to choke on my words.

shallow

Her soul was too deep for him to survive.
A minnow could never withstand an ocean so deep.

sink or swim

So many thoughts running through my mind,
I'm overwhelmed with emotions.
Like a sailboat out at sea,
wind propelling it in every direction.
I feel empty at times and overly full others.
My heart has been ripped apart
too many times to count.
I always manage to stitch it up somehow.
Crazy how I never learned to sew.
My mom taught me right from wrong,
never really teaching me "why" though.
Childhood loneliness anchored my heart-
my dreams and desires too big to imagine.
All I ever wanted was to be loved.
Waiting has always been very difficult for me.
You start to lose hope waiting for something
so long that never materializes- it hurts.
Doubt starts to creep in and everything
you thought you knew, now is a mystery.
Disappointments can leave scars
that make life almost unbearable.
Where do you go when your destiny
is behind a locked door?
You ultimately take any path you
find to be saved from these troubled
waters and they all lead you to
the same place...NOWHERE.

fairytales

She treads on a path, into a future unknown-
this world, not easy to forgive.
Brave without armor, a heart made of stone-
so desperately wanting to live.
Wishes float by, like leaves in the wind-
she watches them dance through the air.
Too quick to catch, she no longer tries-
accepting defeat without reason to care.
Dreams pouring down, from the heavens above-
like waterfalls from the sky.
She stops to drink, from God's fountain of tears,
and listens as his angels cry.
Hopes kiss her lips, sweet like snowflakes,
on a cold winter's day.
Unlike in fairytales, one blink of an eye,
and quickly they fade away.
Love fills her soul, each step of the way,
on this journey of heartache and pain.
With each breath that she takes, it is God
who provides, comfort and shelter from rain.
Written For: Ms. Heaven Maraja

fallen

Have you ever fallen in love with yourself?
You really must try it sometime.
For when you finally understand that the love
we all seek to find in others
has been within ourselves since day one,
the result is remarkably empowering.
NOBODY CAN LOVE YOU, LIKE YOU CAN.

blessing in disguise

You set my soul on fire,
With your handsome face and charming clichés.
Now I'm lost amidst the blaze,
Burned past the point of no return.
Nothing left, merely ashes in an urn.
When will I ever f****** learn?
These men will never change their ways.
Why would they, when we are begging them to stay?
Causing heartbreak while they split their love three ways,
So you swallow pride more than the games they live to play.
There's not enough minutes in a day,
More like a hundred thousand hours.
Reliving each hard truth I learned from cowards.
Their sweet words so fake I've never tasted anything so sour.
Their insides so ugly God will never bless them his power.
Till one day they will see the pain,
Their infidelities scarred women, now beautifully insane.
Forced to find her strength while walking in the rain,
Now their souls on fire from a different type of flame.
One only wisdom will ignite when you release the need to blame.
This story doesn't have to end the same.
Trust actions, not words before you even know their name.
It is you that has control,
Over your enemies who long to steal your soul.
For all them lies, karma dished them up a feast.
Now the tables turn on them like a psychedelic beast.
For the countless times my heart's been broke,
They eat with starving ignorance,
as the poison makes them choke.
Gasping for air, they beg for mercy suffocating from
the smoke.
She now can see her future in the distance-
an epiphany provoked.
A conscious choice she makes to LIVE, A life with God who
blessed her heart with ENDLESS love to give.

the greatest love of all

For as long as I can remember, I've always needed to be heard.
Not just for random acquaintances to read some of my words.
Much more than that.
I envision an audience of 10 million or more.
Bleeding love onto paper and watching it soar across the sky
in a paper airplane aimed for the wastebasket.
Hanging on to my every word with a "death grip."
Opening up the minds and hearts of innocent criminals and
deviant Christians.
Allowing the abundance of love I carry within my soul to
radiate throughout the universe.
Its bright light reaching the darkest of disgusting secrets;
the dirtiest of upstairs closets.
When we speak with loving words and write with the purest
of intentions, the capacity to heal mankind's self-inflicted
wounds is immeasurable.

shine

She no longer would
conform to a mold
of their understanding,
or make choices
at their discretion.
Her obedience was
misconstrued as ignorance.
Silly boys, so quick to assume.
She always knew she
had a hidden trove
of precious jewels
buried deep within her...
...and now it was time
to show them off.

bounce

...and she vowed to herself, the next time a man spoke the
words, "don't worry, I will never leave you,"
that she wouldn't turn and walk away-
she would run as fast as her legs would carry her.
Because her heart was too fragile to risk being slaughtered
by casual nevers, tossed around so carelessly like a rubber ball,
as if she had never played this game before...

the time is now

I didn't want to close the door on you completely,
for fear of forgetting where your wickedness led me.
You tried to control me with trickery and lies-
manipulating my innocent mind by whispering sweet
nothings in my ear.
So naive, I followed your lead- time after agonizing time.
Losing material possessions was never enough to shut you
out and stop chasing your false security I craved so much.
I thought I had found myself in your illusion of love and
excitement, that ended up crashing down every time, like a
shattered mirror falling to the ground.
As my hands dripped with the same blood you flowed
through, scrambling to pick up the broken pieces from the
floor, I COULD FINALLY SEE......
the time had come to close the door, and throw away the
key.

vanity

One day you will see, the colors of my soul.
The truth will find you weeping like a willow tree-
majestic and strong, beautiful from every angle.
Never revealing your hard layers or tangled roots.
Possessing vanity is merely grasping for the wind.
Living in truth will set you free.

speechless

It isn't often I'm at a loss for words.
It's different this time, this day.
For I have achieved my dream.
Nothing will stand in my way.

A bright future lies ahead of me.
No more worrying about the past.
For once I claimed victory,
It was impossible to finish last.

my savior

There is a light emerging from within my soul.
It glimmers like gold dust from an angel's wing.
God speaks from within me. I hear his voice tell me that
strength lives abundantly,
where my darkest fears reside.
He offered me courage when the enemy convinced me
I was destined to fail, not worthy of a life without struggle or strife.
Never could I have made it here on my own.
It is the love of Jesus that carries me to every destination.

love is me

I am inspired by beauty in its purest forms.
People with genuine hearts and faces
wearing nothing but a smile.
Sunsets where the sun literally melts into the
ocean so blue.
Flowers with petals missing from its perfect symmetry,
showing we get more beautiful as we age.
Birds that fly across the sky with grace as their
wings stay still as can be.
Skies filled with endless mysteries beyond the
stars they flaunt each night.
Children who laugh uncontrollably as they swing as
high as the chains will carry them.
Butterflies of all colors who seem to almost say hello
before they fly off on their journey.
Nothing inspires me more than love, however.
Love is the most beautiful of all these.
I am love.
Love is me.

mind control

Dreams as big as the sky- fears not far behind.
It's a race to survive; a pot of gold we all seek to find.
A simple thought can trip and fall on it's way to the finish line.
Seek the truth when lies lost in dust are merely diamonds
that have yet to be shined.
Taught to believe in myself, first and foremost.
Not once was my best even close.
Take a chance and chase your dreams,
is what we've conditioned our minds.
If you fall, get right back up and don't stop
till you run out of time.
Lighting crashes down, when you least expect it to rain.
Love turns to hate, like fire on ice bleeding pain.
Trust that life will pass you by, if time should ever stand still.
Looking back can't change the past,
so don't think you control how you feel.

hard work pays off

Along the way I learned to thy self always stay true.
When you pretend to be someone else
the only person who hurts is YOU.
Don't look for handouts, especially when the arm
it's attached to might be Lucifer's limb.
Stop comparing yourself to others
whom haven't walked a day in your shoes.
Fancy feet always stay clean
when they never get put to good use.
If you are working hard towards your goals everyday,
then that's all that truly matters.
It's your future.
Make it bright.

god's gifts

A broken heart, a soul of shame, blue eyes that can't hide pain.
An empty glass, dark grey sky, no umbrella when it rains.
Scattered ash, melted wax, the lampshade that got burned.
A rose with thorns, an empty vase, lessons still not learned.
Silver-plate, man made gems, a finger with no ring.
Lifeless trees, dead brown leaves, birds that can not sing.
Forgotten wishes, broken dreams, a future without hope.
Goodbye letters, blank white paper, no stamp on the envelope.
All of these things, God created, for us here on Earth.
It's up to us, to love enough, so we can see their worth.

looking back

I look back on all the time I had to
waste, All the smiles I was forced
to fake, Those glasses of wine I
was so eager to taste, All those
trials life pushed me to face.
I think back on all those lessons
I had to learn, All those men who
devoured my heart in one bite,
Those dresses I wore with intent
to make men yearn, All those pens
who didn't share their ink so I
could write.
I look back on all the gray skies
that could have been blue,
On those nights I should have
been in your arms, On all those
lies that could never be true,
On all the fights I surrendered to
your charm.
I look back on all my broken
hearts I was forced to mend,
All those tears I had to cry,
All those rules I broke but tried to
bend, All those times you said you
loved me but you lied.
After looking back on all these
things that haunt me from the
past, I'm grateful for each and
every one, For the peace it brings
at last, To know that in the end, I
WON.

no more ink

I picked up a pen this morning,
so I could write my pain away.
I tried to write but nothing would come out.
The paper was still blank.
I couldn't figure out where my words disappeared to.
Did they up and walk away?
Were they ever really there?
Was my hand broken?
Maybe my mind was in a fog.
I started to panic, but didn't break a sweat.
How ironic, my pen had no more ink.
Good thing I didn't call for help.
For a moment I almost thought I had lost my voice.
No, never that.

CPSIA information can be obtained
at www.ICGtesting.com
Printed in the USA
FSHW020501180919
62132FS